LOCKED & LOADED

BY DANIEL PENALOZA

Word From The Author:

This collection of poetry, inspirational quotes, and original literary art comes from the mind and soul of a man that's fought against all odds and wagers that were stacked against him in life. Regardless of what life throws at you, hold your ground, stay strong, and keep calm. With time you will see the naysayers disappear, the haters will steer clear, and the rest will be consumed by disbelief and anger filled tears. Pray for them …

TABLE OF CONTENTS

TABLE OF CONTENTS

THE MAIN ENTRÉES

Caliber

Individuals in your life may come & go, much
like the tides of the oceans that flow in, High
and low.

Misconception and manipulation, resonate
upon naive and foolish ears,

leaving a taste of the fowl caliber ingested

from that person causing trust issues & fears.

Choose wisely the caliber of people you

associate yourself with,

Don't get left looking stupid, dysfunctional,

with no one wanting to hear about this...

I feel like a dark blue Indigo Snake, that resides & dwells in the lush forests of Fla; my home state,

A cross between purple and aquatic blue, a color tone that I always favor since I go thru life in stealth mode, with no one having a clue.

A blend of darkness with aquatic ties, no one is perfect, but this color helps stagnate and delay any release of irrelevant information or untold lies.

Deception & unfinished facts of information is not my forte, yet being misunderstood leaves me leaning towards this dark shade of secrecy, pushing discussions for a later time and a much more appropriate place.

During the day I will always be transparent & clear, when night falls upon us, don't question me, follow the Indigo river left behind, I will always be near...

I remain calm like the water,
poised for that triggering noise.

Be lead by your wisdom, it's not
in your best interest, make the
right choice...

Locked & Loaded

I travel thru life with a single setting,
"Locked & Loaded",#alwaysf$ckingready.
Be fully aware that if conflict arises, this is
your warning, proceed with caution, what
you don't know maybe fatally harming.

I favor the quiet, calm, unpredictable
approach towards those who bark at me.
Gather yourself fool, prior to engaging in
conflict against me. I favor no methods on
how things get done, in the court room,
through collateral damage, any option is
best vs. having to choose the caliber of my
gun.

Melancholy

I wake up wondering where & why this
sadness follows me from day to day.
Am I mourning from a lost family member or
is it an Ex that lingers in my thoughts and is
here to stay.
I can't explain, why I feel the way I do, I've
tried medicine, counseling and neither of
those options are coming through.
I finally seek God for a spiritual answer &
insight, and pray for discipline so I can live life
drama free with no worries of being engaged
constantly in fights.
I will keep praying to God for closure, while
he helps me control my feelings & govern my
composure...

All they ask from us is honesty, trust & respect.

Some of us provide it with ease, while others lie, pretend & steal hearts like thieves.
"Melancholy"...

Dig•ni•ty

The state or quality of being worthy of honor or respect. At birth we are granted this thru our innocence.

As adults we gain or lose this based on life decisions.

The goal is to carry yourself consistently in life within its realm...

cour•age
The ability to do something that frightens one.

Each and everyone of us possess a degree of
this. Some exaggerate and portray more than
what lies within.
Stay real, always.
Approach every challenge or conflict in life
with a level of courage that reflects who you
are, not what you claim to be.

COURAGE IS INSTILLED &
EMBRACED DURING
CHILDHOOD.

DIGNITY HONOR & RESPECT
IS EARNED THRU LIFE.

Mood killer, mood killer, mood killer,
things people say, things people do, things
people wear to get attention, do they even
have a clue?
The scent you give off, or the way you smell,
are looked over and forgiven by
friends & family, but others wonder, "what
the hell" ?
Text messages ending with acronyms like
SMH or TMI, should hint at the fact that you're
"killing my mood" , please don't cross that
line, is that understood ?
If communication becomes limited or, "I'm too
busy right now let's talk another time", is
expressed.
Analyse the dialogue exchanged & maybe you
will realize the true reasons behind my
responses & why I don't need that stress...
"mood killer"

Cyanide

There are family members, lovers & friends
that will evoke toxicity into your life. "cyanide"
Unwilling you will digest & be exposed to this
poisonous experience.
It will be up to you to confront it, handle it, or
just change it's appearance.
With time it will consume you, make you ill,
and even take your last breath.
Mimicking an addicts indulgence & craving of
a lethal injection from a dose of Meth...
"cyanide"

Dark Horse

A candidate or competitor about whom little is know, but who unexpectedly wins or succeeds.

This is my trait of choice, I'm not one to brag, bolster or talk in a loud voice.

I analyse, compose & strategically plan my moves in life, much like a scalpel is positioned and angled for a precision slice.

I keep my accomplishments & accolades a secret from most, only to reveal, celebrate and rejoice with people that I trust and keep close.

Never underestimate me during a confrontation, I will leave you numb, delusional, confused and filled with frustration...

"dark horse"

Like a shadow in the night, I structure strategies for my next strike

Never feel confidence thru controlling my reins, darkness & rage is constantly flowing thru my veins.

"Dark Horse"

Whiskey

Take some shots, thou fear not, It's hot a$s hell outside,
make that a double on the rocks.
It goes down smooth & quick, I suddenly begin to feel Ill and
somewhat sick.
I nonchalantly walk towards the bathroom halls, trip over
my laces, and slam face first into an oncoming wall.
I recover, compose myself , afraid to even look around.
I feel like total a$s, a moron or better said a drunk and
pathetic clown.
I seldom drink, but felt the need to this day, here I am
worshiping the porcelain gods,
left wondering how long I will be feeling this way...
"whiskey"

Falling prey to the demons of addiction is common.

It's what you stand to lose that should instill self discipline within you, "whiskey"...

Rem•i•nisce

To indulge in enjoyable recollection of past events

I reminisce about how life once was. The people and places that have crossed my path. It's been a journey thru a lush forest. At times I've had to use a machete, cutting through vines & thick brush, solely to reach the destination I desire. I often risk creating a new pathway in life, the ones most commonly traveled by don't always appeal to my lifestyle or beliefs.

Razor Blades

Dwelling on some past misfortune, while jamming out to some tracks from Frank Ocean,
I ponder on how some things went down,
So many years lost, never to be renewed much less found.
Shredded hearts, sliced up feelings, all commingled simultaneously and left bleeding.
Misconceived thoughts & demeanors will dwell for eternity,
Open wounds & scars will leave inexplicable pain, far worse than maternity...

I've been thinking, contemplating, almost to the point of drinking. New year, my mind is clear, definitely shifting gears, faster with fury unlike the previous years. I'm focused more than ever, It's like T. Edison inventing something new and shouting out "now that's clever".

It's amazing when you have the right people in your life. Who knows, I might even be close to finding a wife.

I must be

I must be blind to realize, what I hold inside. At times I wonder who am I, and what am I capable of. Feeling clueless and still finding myself, I'm left checking none of the above and not much else. I finally wake up from this bad dream, recover, awaken and then come clean. I must be on earth for a purpose, I thank you God for assisting me in not feeling worthless.

Lust

The devil prays on most men with this. He sends his army of enticing women to deliver acts of bliss.

The weak & promiscuous indulge in this regularly, while the devil watches, laughs and shakes his head at thee.

Lust is a hidden feature in some of us, controlling, resisting and standing your ground is extremely hard, but a needed must.

You will never keep a good woman in your life, much less ever land a beautiful wife.

Gasoline laced streets, ignition source is triggered, Fuego is established.

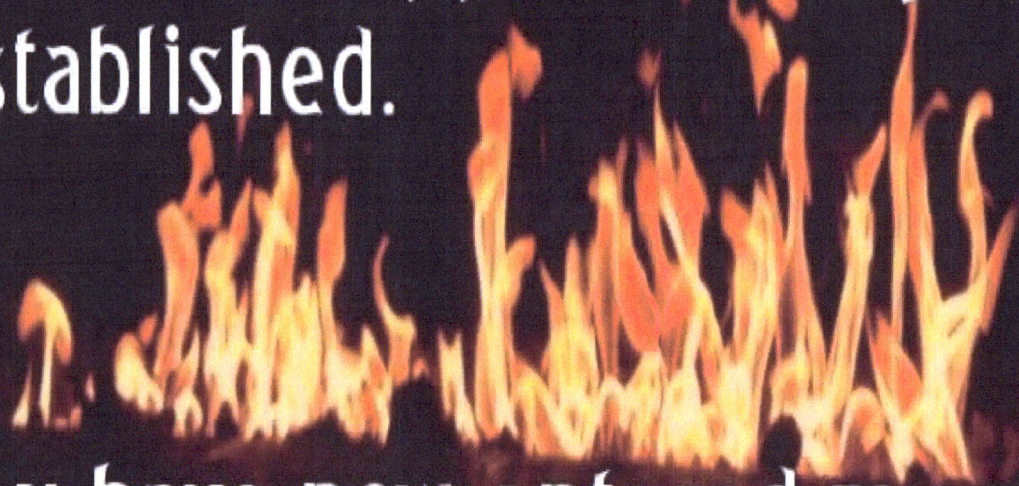

You have now entered my ring of fire, odds of escaping have become obsolete, thoughts of survival, #bleak

Anonymous

Anonymously I venture thru the night, with my haters constantly watching my every move and keeping me in their sights,

I sometimes question if they have a life, it is clear they are more focused on me than potentially finding a wife.

I laugh at such immature behavior, I pray to God they come to their senses and seek their savior. Obsession is a sickness derived from dysfunction. Oops, did I just say that, yes I do believe I just structured a conjunction...

Novacane

Venturing thru life there are people, places & things that will leave you numb, "Novacane". In turn there are people, places & things you will instill numbness onto, "Novacane". Collaterally, confusion, regret, & remorse,

will set in and take it's course.

Always view things from a larger than life spectrum, turning back may be too late & the consequences will be too much to handle and then some. "Novacane"...

Laying amongst the pines, I intertwine, blend in, come to a coil, & begin to align.

Turn away cautiously, I will bring you loss of sensation & death derived from curiosity.

Missing you

I miss having your 98.6° next to me.

Even though we just met, it feels like destiny was already set. Your unique ways, and tantalizing voice, all sum up that I've made the right choice. I count down the days until we meet, waiting restlessly to kiss those lips that are forever sweet...

WARRIOR

I WAKE UP EVERY DAY, LICKING MY WOUNDS,
ANALYSING MY BRUISES, WHILE FOCUSING ON MY
NEXT PREY.

I DON'T SEEK BATTLES AGAINST THE GOOD. ITS
THOSE THAT ARE AGAINST ME OR HAVE ME
MISUNDERSTOOD.

I TAKE ON EVERY CHALLENGE ONE BY ONE, MAKING
THEM WONDER HOW I SURVIVE, WITH LITTLE FOOD,
HARDLY ANY WATER & A GLIMPSE OF SUN.

I HOLD MY GROUND AND REMAIN SOLID AS A ROCK,
PUNCHES THROWN ARE BLOCKED IN HAND TO HAND
COMBAT, LEAVING THEM NO OTHER OPTIONS BUT THE
GLOCK.

MOST FRICTION OFTEN EXCEEDS NORMAL
EXPECTATIONS, WITH THE BATTLE ENDING IN
SURREAL CONTEMPLATION...

"WARRIOR"

Beast Mode

It's over 100 degrees, and my body is feeling
weak. My muscles are locking up & the
outcome is looking bleak.

Then I realize what it took to get here, many
sacrifice blood, sweat & tears, and still never
come this near

"Beast mode", some of us excel physically
and achieve this state of mind,

while others claim to reach it without
experiencing intensity and exertion for long
periods of time.

You will come across many that "talk the
talk", but few that will actually "walk the
walk", keep it real, "beast mode"...

Dear lord, I pray to you night & day, I assure you my faith is rock solid, even though it comes off as fray.

I know you will answer all my prayers, maybe not today, maybe not tomorrow, but I know you love me & truly care...

Note to self

I just woke up, it was a crazy night, I'm still feeling fu#$ed up, noticing bruises, did I just get in a fight?

I forgot to take the dog out and now my carpet is a mess, my fiancée just broke up with me and she is returning the dress.

"Note to self", I better get my sh&t together before I and up dead.

My brother is in jail & my sisters pregnant, from my long lost cousin named Fred ?

Dear lord have mercy, I just noticed I smashed into my garage door, after killing my neighbors cat named "Percy", guess she won't be eating anymore of that "Adore".

"Note to self", this all must be a bad dream, dammit I can't ever go back to that bar or get caught up in that scene.

I reach for my scalp & realize I'm wearing a wig & dress. Lord what have I become, a drag queen that looks like a hot mess?

"Note to self", all this partying must come to an end, before I end up in jail and become Juan & Tyrone's best friend...

RUNNING

SOME OF US FIND OURSELVES RUNNING FROM THE PAST
& AT TIMES FROM THE PRESENT EVEN THOUGH WE HAD
A BLAST.
NOTHING EVER SEEMS TO LAST, SOCIETY AS A HOLE IS
ALWAYS ON A MAD DASH. WHAT HAPPENED TO
PATIENCE AND DUE PROCESS.
THIS DEFICIENCY IN TODAY'S SOCIETY, STRIKES MANY
OF US AS SHEER NONSENSE,
KEEP YOUR COMPOSURE, RUNNING IS NOT A MUST, PACE
YOURSELF, DON'T RUN OUT OF BREATH, INVEST IN WHO
YOU TRUST...

Taboo

Met this girl one day at a Starbucks
establishment. I found her cute, sexy,
somewhat nerdy & with a foreign accent.
A conversation began, dialog was exchanged,
at that time I knew my thoughts would never
be the same.
A metamorphosis took place in my heart &
soul. A tall physique, long legs and a petite
short torso.
She came across as a forbidden fruit, I
became nervous, anxious, leaving me no
choice but to loosen my tie & unbutton my
suit.
I normally never gravitate to women of this
type, yet looking around, both women and
men have kept her in their sight.
As I begin to leave I wish her a blessed day,
by the way my name is Drew, and please
don't take this the wrong way.
I find you extremely enticing and attractive,
I'm sure you hear that often, forgive me if
you're offended, I'm not seeking to be
sexually active.
"Taboo"

Wake up everyday, stand for who you are, always be on guard.

Confronting me is a mistake, you will get scarred, heed this warning near & far. I back down from no one, it's irrelevant to me who you are.

Sugar & Spice

An exceptional evening with my Diamond laced Pocahontas. A modern day version of Aphrodite, the Greek goddess.

I invite her into my abode, without hesitation she accepts, my heartbeat intensifies, my soul transitions, falling into erotic mode.

She enters and her curvaceous outline is displayed by her shadow, it sends a burning sensation through my skin, no need for Aloe.

I reach for her wrist, delicately pull her towards me, she turns with anticipated intentions and wraps herself around me. She initiates a methodical kiss, I reciprocate her actions & seductively indulge on her lips. The flavor of her gloss strikes me, "sugar & spice". I then realize I'm playing with fire, should I even care to roll the dice.

The arousing flavor takes over me, I pick her up & place her on my kitchen counter, her body language confirms this was expected but would complicate the encounter. The passionate exchange of emotions cease. Thoughts of a fisherman's ethics overwhelm me, "catch & release".

I place her back down, she whispers "it's too soon". I nod and concur, walk her out, then watch her pull away as I'm left gazing at the moon...

I'M 4'2" & PACK A PUNCH
DON'T BE FOOLED I'LL TAKE
YOU OUT & EAT YOUR
LUNCH.

STEP BACK FOOL, WATCH
YOURSELF, ONCE I LAND
THIS RIGHT HAND YOU'LL
BECOME LIFELESS, NUMB,
FALL TO YOUR KNEES, NOT
MUCH ELSE.